Original title:
Seeds of Truth

Copyright © 2025 Creative Arts Management OÜ
All rights reserved.

Author: Sophia Kingsley
ISBN HARDBACK: 978-1-80567-037-7
ISBN PAPERBACK: 978-1-80567-117-6

Nurturing the Seedling

In the garden of wisdom we plant with care,
With laughter and giggles dancing in the air.
A quirky little sprout peeks out with a grin,
Hoping to grow with a cheeky spin.

We water our dreams with a splash and a joke,
A humorous tune for the soil to soak.
The worms have a laugh, wiggling with glee,
They wiggle and squirm, as silly as can be.

A sunshine ray beams with a wink from above,
"Grow tall, little sprout! You're destined to love!"
The daisies all giggle as they sway in the breeze,
While the bees buzz a tune, putting all minds at ease.

Each petal that blossoms brings joy to the day,
While squirrels form a band and sing out in play.
So nurture your seedlings with laughter and cheer,
In this garden of giggles, there's nothing to fear.

What Lies Beneath

In the garden of fibs and tales,
Worms wiggle, with their little scales.
They gossip, whisper with quite a zeal,
While carrots wonder what's the real deal.

Turnips turn up their leafy hats,
'Who told the beans they could be such brats?'
Underneath the soil, oh what a riot,
Truths dig in deep, but are too shy to try it.

The Unseen Harvest

In the field of giggles, what do we reap?
Surprises sprout from secrets we keep.
A pumpkin who dreams of becoming a pie,
Says 'I'm more than a veggie, just give it a try!'

The corn cackles softly, a kernel full of jest,
Plotting a prank that it thinks is the best.
When the moon's out, they throw a ball,
With dance moves that make even weeds have a sprawl.

Blossoming Perceptions

A daisy claims it sees the light,
But a sunflower says, 'You're just too tight!'
With petals bright, they argue and play,
Over who's first to greet the day.

But beneath the bickering blooms a stare,
Of misshapen truths beyond compare.
In laughter, they twist in a sunny embrace,
Finding joy in the quirks of their space.

Fertile Truths

In a garden where laughter grows so wide,
There's a tomato who's been on quite the ride.
'Thought I was ripe, but turns out I'm green!
Guess I'll just wait for a salad, how mean!'

A cucumber chuckles, leaning on the fence,
'Truths are like pickles; they can be intense!'
With a wink, the veggies play tag till it's dark,
Chasing the sprout with a joke and a spark.

Whispers Beneath the Surface

In a garden full of chatter,
The carrots wish to sing.
But all the other plants just giggle,
Saying, 'What could they bring?'

Beneath the earth they plot and scheme,
While worms dance through the muck.
'Our wisdom's rooted deep,' they beam,
'But we need a little luck!'

The Quiet Growth of Knowledge

In a pot sat a sage old bean,
Reading books under the sun.
'You think I'm just a simple scene?
My thoughts are never done!'

The herbs were rolling their green eyes,
Saying, 'What's a bean to do?'
But as they whispered, oh so sly,
They learned a bit or two!

Dreams Buried in Soil

A cabbage had a quirky dream,
To dance beneath the moon.
While radishes just laughed and schemed,
'You can't! You're stuck till June!'

But overnight it turned out right,
The cabbage twirled with glee.
From beneath the soil, in the night,
It found sweet liberty!

Beneath the Canopy of Certainty

Underneath the mighty tree,
The acorns made a vow.
'We'll grow like giants, wait and see!
Though we're tiny hip-hop now.'

The leaves above just swayed and sighed,
'What nonsense! We're the truth!'
But little nuts dug deep and tried,
To prove their own sweet youth!

The Unseen Harvest

In the garden of thought, where giggles sprout,
We plant little whispers, without a doubt.
A turnip of wisdom, a carrot of jest,
Harvesting laughter, we truly are blessed.

Cabbages chuckle, while radishes grin,
Every veggie's a scholar, let the fun begin!
With compost of quirks and a sprinkle of cheer,
The unseen harvest brings us all near.

Shadows of Enlightenment

In the shadows so deep, where wisdom plays,
We dance with the quirks in hilarious ways.
A shadowy figure with a hat that's too wide,
Tells jokes to the moon, on this whimsical ride.

Giggling ghosts whisper truths from the past,
Their punchlines are hidden, but fun's always fast.
As laughter seeps out from the cracks of the dark,
Enlightenment shines with a ridiculous spark.

Threads of Reality

Weaving the fabric of oddities bright,
Threads of perception twirl left and right.
The needle's a riddle, the chart's a perplex,
We stich up the nonsense with laughter, what's next?

A tapestry tangled where giggles unite,
We question the fabric, with a wink and a bite.
In this quirky creation, the truth is a dance,
A performative jest, golden threads in a trance.

Sprouts of Insight

In the sunny backyard of our playful mind,
Tiny sprouts of insight, all twisted and blind.
A cucumber's pondering the ways of the pea,
"Why can't we just roll? Oh, that's the key!"

Radical roots reach for the clouds overhead,
Spreading opinions like butter on bread.
With giggles and glee, let's water this plot,
For sprouts of insight can't help but be hot!

Nature's Whispered Realities

In the garden of giggles, we play,
Plants gossip softly, come what may.
Butterflies flutter, with secrets they keep,
While worms wear spectacles, counting their sheep.

Beneath the big oak, a squirrel's lost sleep,
He swears he heard rocks in a pile, take a leap.
Daisies be laughing, swaying with glee,
While moles dig tunnels for their own jamboree.

Cultivated by Time

With hands in the soil, a mess to create,
A pickle jar holds wisdom, don't underestimate.
Each weed has a story, each bug has a name,
While the carrots keep laughing, at broccoli's fame.

The sun pulls a trick, with shadows that dance,
While tumbleweeds rolling, go for a chance.
Old fence posts whisper of lovers long gone,
And daisies pretend they know every yawn.

Tilling the Mind's Soil

In the field of thoughts, we plant a few laughs,
Watered by giggles, not just the haphazard halves.
Crows caw confessions, while squirrels throw shade,
On the ripe, juicy vegetables that sun has made.

Composting our secrets, turning old tales,
While radishes snicker at narrow-gauged trails.
Amidst the tall corn, a scarecrow does sway,
And mumbles wisecracks about yesterday's hay.

Deeper Than the Surface

Digging down deeper, we found a potato,
His jokes about onions, a true comedy show.
With dirt on our noses, we laugh and we cheer,
While sprouts play charades, pretending to fear.

The rabbits are jesters, with ears oh so grand,
Hopping with glee, like they've just made a band.
With seeds of laughter, we sow and we reap,
In this garden of nonsense, we'll never lose sleep.

Budding Realizations

In a garden of giggles, wisdom grows,
With carrots of insight, and broccoli prose.
The radishes chuckle, while onions agree,
That the funniest truths hide behind leafy tea.

The daisies whisper secrets, silly and bright,
While clovers do cartwheels, a humorous sight.
A tomato claims it's the juiciest one,
But a squash just rolls by, laughing and fun.

As leaves rustle gently, they dance to a tune,
The berries are buzzing, a laugh in full bloom.
In this patch of nonsense where knowledge is neat,
Truth wears a comical hat, isn't that sweet?

And as we dig deep in that fertile patch,
We find giggling facts in a vibrant mismatch.
So let's plant our laughter, let's water with glee,
For in this light-heartedness, we all can agree.

Truths Hidden in Petals

A flower with humor, it blooms with a grin,
Its petals are tickled by breezes of sin.
The bees are all buzzing, they're cracking a joke,
While the roses just chuckle, their laughter bespoke.

Daffodils waltz, with a burst of pure cheer,
They spread silly tales that everyone hears.
With tulips in tutus performing a skit,
All hidden truths dance, and we laugh at the wit.

A sunflower whispers, "I'm tall for a reason!"
The daisies reply, "It's all about season!"
While violets giggle, their colors so rare,
In this bouquet of jest, truth's unraveling flair.

So join in the chaos, let's giggle and sway,
For every petal hides wisdom in play.
In this garden so raucous, where laughter refines,
We find honesty wrapped in nature's designs.

Echoes of the Past

Once in a meadow, a tale was spun,
Of mischief and folly, oh what witty fun!
The squirrels chattered, recounting their plight,
How they mistook acorns for shiny delights.

An old tree reminisced, while leaning with glee,
About saplings who giggled, 'Oh look at me!'
The shadows retold stories of laughter's embrace,
As sunlight peeked in, lighting up every face.

The wind swung by, sharing secrets with trees,
Of silly mistakes that brought everyone these:
Like frogs in smart hats debating the rain,
Echoes of laughter, a humorous chain.

So let's listen closely, to these voices of yore,
Find joy in each giggle, and learn to adore.
In the whispers of nature, in memories vast,
We uncover the folly, and truths that will last.

Awakening Authenticity

With each silly wiggle, the truth starts to shake,
As we dance through the meadows, all laughter awake.
The daisies declare they prefer polka dots,
While the tulips insist on outrageous thoughts.

A butterfly flutters with style and flair,
It says, "Be a fool! No reason to care!"
The grasshoppers hop with their own little jazz,
And the whole world joins in, saying, "What a raz!"

Amidst all the giggles, the realness is found,
In jests and in banter, where joy does abound.
The daisies in hats and the bees with their glee,
Are the essence of growth, wild and totally free.

So let's awaken to laughter, let nonsense collide,
For in truth's funny mirror, the heart opens wide.
In the garden of whimsy, in each playful scene,
We find our true self in the spaces in-between.

The Tapestry of Honesty

Threads of honesty weave so bright,
They twirl and dance in playful light.
But watch your step, it's quite a sight,
As truth gets tangled, oh what a fright!

Lies are like weeds in a garden fair,
Sprouting up without a care.
Pull them out, if you dare,
Or soon you'll have quite the hairy affair!

Each stitch holds stories, some quite absurd,
Like chickens that gossip, oh how they've stirred!
If truth's a bird, then lies are a herd,
Flying in circles, haven't you heard?

So grab your scissors, cut through the haze,
Unravel those threads in a comical craze.
For honesty's tapestry is full of plays,
And laughter will guide us through quirky maze.

Germination of Insights

In the garden of thoughts, ideas sprout,
With sunshine and giggles, they dance about.
Water them well, don't twist and shout,
For facts can wiggle, and wiggles can flout!

Imagine a bulb that takes a long nap,
Dreaming of wisdom, snug in its wrap.
When it finally wakes, it maps out a gap,
And starts handing out advice on a funny mishap!

When truths collide, oh what a scene!
Like squirrels debating over last night's cuisine.
Who ate the nuts? Was it Dan or Christine?
The outcome was messy, sticky, yet clean!

So plant those laughs in your mind's very soil,
Let them germinate with each giggle and toil.
When insights bloom, they do so in oil,
Frying our doubts, all the nonsense we spoil.

Delicate Roots of Reality

Beneath our feet lie secrets and lies,
Roots that giggle and sometimes cry.
If thoughts were plants, oh my, oh my,
They'd tangle and giggle, reach for the sky!

The truth wears a crown of leafy disguise,
But roots have their reasons and clever replies.
Ask them a question, and they'll tell you why,
The world's a circus, undertruths fly!

Worms wriggle, and whispers seem grand,
Fables and tales toss around like a band.
Plant your doubts, give 'em a hand,
You might find humor where roots stand!

So dig deep down, through muck and through mire,
To find the truth that never tires.
Where giggles stay hidden, and laughter inspires,
Reality's roots are tangled in choir.

What the Ground Conceals

The ground is a thief, oh what a tease,
It hides the gossip with utter ease.
What's buried beneath? Who knows? Just please,
Let's dig it up, like some ancient cheese!

Moles wear spectacles, plotting a scheme,
To uncover the tales that float like a dream.
With every shovel, they chuckle and beam,
What's hidden below? It's quite the supreme!

Worms crack jokes about dirt and its charms,
While roots throw parties with all of their arms.
Yet trying to grasp what the underground farms,
Can lead to a mess of bizarre alarms!

So let's tiptoe softly, let's peek and explore,
What the ground conceals behind its door.
With laughter as our guide, we'll dance on the floor,
And uncover the secrets we all can adore!

The Tapestry of Belief

In a garden of laughs, the colors collide,
Where whispers of insight and chuckles reside.
We plant little questions, like sprouting vines,
Tickling our minds with their funny designs.

A tree of odd notions, all twisted and bent,
With branches of laughter, we merrily spent.
Each leaf holds a tale, slightly absurd,
As we giggle aloud at the truths we inferred.

Unraveling the Mysteries

With each twist and turn, we discover delight,
A sock in the wash, a cat in mid-flight.
Tying our thoughts into knots of pure fun,
The mysteries linger till we're all done.

A puzzle of quips, with pieces astray,
We laugh at our questions—will they ever obey?
In a world full of quirks, let's dance in the shade,
Where answers may hide, but good jokes are made.

Illuminated Paths of Discovery

A flashlight of humor, we wander about,
Discovering paths where the giggles shout.
Each step is a riddle, a playful surprise,
Bright lights of nonsense flash before our eyes.

Like fireflies twinkling, our thoughts come to play,
As we wander the woods of the funny array.
The shadows may tease, but we've nothing to fear,
For madness is clear when the laughter draws near.

Sowing the Unknown

With hands in the dirt, we mix joy and jest,
Planting odd fables, a curious quest.
Watering dreams with a sprinkle of cheer,
As the seedlings of whims begin to appear.

In rows of absurdity, we tend with delight,
Our garden of giggles grows tall and takes flight.
Each bloom tells a story, all wacky and wild,
Where nonsense and wisdom dance, laughing like a child.

The Silent Growth

In the garden, quiet lies,
Wiggling roots wear no disguise.
The whispers of the soil speak,
To the buds that gently peek.

Worms parade with a squishy dance,
In muddy boots, they take a chance.
They twist and turn with tiny glee,
As flowers giggle, 'Look at me!'

The daisies try to tell a joke,
But bees just buzz and start to poke.
The puns are sweet, the laughter blooms,
While sunbeams warm the leafy rooms.

Yet all the while beneath the sun,
Little truths are sprouting fun.
With every chuckle from the ground,
A playful wisdom can be found.

Blossoms of Awareness

In patches bright and colors bold,
A line of daisies, tales retold.
Awareness tickles like a breeze,
As squirrels giggle from the trees.

The tulips sport their fancy hats,
While ants march under leafy mats.
With every bloom, a secret shared,
Of all the follies, none are spared.

The garden party's in full swing,
With every petal, laughter's king.
They dance, they sway, in joyful cheer,
The tangled vines hug everyone near.

Oh, listen close, the flowers sing,
Of silly truths that joy can bring.
A symphony of green and gold,
Awareness blooms in hugs so bold.

Beneath the Surface Lies Gold

A patch of dirt, so oh-so plain,
Where grumpy flowers complain and strain.
But peek below with curious eyes,
And find a treasure in disguise.

Moles are digging with such delight,
Uncovering truths that shine so bright.
While daisies mock, the roots grow deep,
In the riddle where secrets sleep.

Each weed's a figure dressed in green,
Telling tales of what's unseen.
Invisible giggles fill the air,
As nature plays its funny fair.

So cherish what's buried, don't despair,
In every clump, a truth to bear.
With humor sprouting in the fold,
Beneath the surface, lies the gold.

The Sprouting of Clarity

In the greenhouse, jokes take root,
As clarity wears a clownish suit.
With every sprout, a punchline's born,
As lettuce leaves laugh 'til they're worn.

Carrots burrow beneath the gloom,
While radishes share their bubbly boom.
The sunbeams wink, the shadows twirl,
In the veggie patch, giggles unfurl.

All sprouts are dancing, what a sight,
In silliness, they find their light.
With roots intertwined in playful cheer,
Each truth emerges, loud and clear.

So when you wander, take some time,
To see the laughter in the rhyme.
For clarity, in jest, appears,
Through sprouting greens and endless cheers.

The Essence of Enlightenment

In a garden so bright, a gnome felt wise,
With a hat full of thoughts, beneath sunny skies.
He pondered deep truths while sipping his tea,
And debated with ants on what it means to be.

A parrot chimed in, with a feathered flair,
Claiming wisdom comes from the length of your hair.
The daisies just giggled, the tulips rolled eyes,
As the gnome tripped and fell, 'Oh, how can this be?'

The sunbeam then winked, saying, "Take it light!"
"Enlightenment sometimes is just a fun flight."
With laughter and joy, they all danced away,
Finding bliss in the chaos, a glorious play.

Awakening the Senses

A tickle of spring made the flowers get dressed,
With petals so bright, they looked truly blessed.
The bees buzzed a tune, while the breeze hummed along,
Ten worms broke into a very short song.

A snail with a shell like a fancy old car,
Said, "Life moves too fast, let's not venture too far!"
He invited his pals for a very slow stroll,
Debating whether cucumbers can play a rock role.

The sun peeked through leaves, looking oh-so divine,
While squirrels pulled pranks on the unsuspecting vine.
"I smell something good!" cried a wise old toad,
"Maybe it's wisdom or maybe it's road!

Nature's Unwritten Stories

In the heart of the woods, a turtle named Ted,
Wove tales of adventure while munching on bread.
He claimed he once raced a rabbit so spry,
Who tripped on a root and whizzed by the sky.

A fox with a grin said, "Let's write a book,
Of squirrels who dance and take photos with rook!"
The owl hooted loud, "Oh, this will be great,
I'll add in a chapter on why we stay late."

The wind whispered secrets, and branches took notes,
Of mischief and laughter from all of their folks.
In the end, they agreed it's best kept a tale,
For stories of laughter can never grow stale.

Insights Among the Wildflowers

Among wildflowers bloomed a quirky bouquet,
Where daisies debated and poppies would sway.
"Let's ponder life's meaning, or maybe just cake?"
Said a curious violet, as petals would shake.

A sunflower sighed, "I'm too tall for this chat,
Why don't you guys try on my giant new hat?"
So they wore it with glee, like a botanical crew,
And concocted a plot to prank old pig, too!

They turned a dull noon into a festival grand,
With laughter as bright as the sun's golden band.
Insights sprung forth from their silly delight,
In the realm of wildflowers, the mood felt just right.

The Elegance of Growth

In the garden of mind, ideas sprout,
Like flowers dancing, no room for doubt.
With a sip of sunshine, a sprinkle of rain,
They wear their brilliance, never complain.

Worms wiggle with flair, teaching us how,
That even the squishy can take a bow.
Petunias giggle with colors so bright,
As the bees buzz around, a comedic sight.

Roots tell a story, ancient and wise,
While dandelion wishes float up to the skies.
A cabbage with pomp dances in the breeze,
Sharing its secrets with the light-hearted leaves.

And in this chaos, where laughter will bloom,
Truths are embedded in each little room.
With a tickle of soil and a pinch of delight,
Growth is the punchline that feels just right.

The Blossoming of Knowing

Petals unfurl like gossiping friends,
Each one a story, as knowledge extends.
In the sunshine's glow, they wiggle and sway,
Caught in a debate about brightening the day.

A sunflower struts in its golden attire,
Claiming it knows how to reach higher.
While daisies conspire, with a wink and a nod,
They whisper sweet secrets from garden to sod.

Butterflies flutter, donning their flair,
Teaching the roses to stop and declare.
'We're not just flowers, let's join in the fun,
With humor and wisdom, we've only begun!'

And in this vineyard of laughable lore,
Each bloom brings a chuckle, like never before.
Joy does the tango, while knowledge will sing,
As nature rolls out her comedic bling.

Fructifying Thoughts

Ideas scatter like fruit from a tree,
Each one a nibble, ripe as can be.
Bananas yell 'slip!' while apples just grin,
In this orchard of wisdom, where smiles begin.

Peaches are plump with a juicy secret,
While lemons just pucker, their humor a treat.
A berry flirts boldly, 'I'm the zest of the bunch!'
Making everyone giggle with a sugary crunch.

In this garden of wit, the pumpkins all laugh,
Planing their heist on the autumnal path.
They plot with the squash, quite a silly brigade,
Sharing their stories, while mischief is played.

So grab your basket, let's gather some cheer,
These thoughts, oh so fruity, are ripe for the year.
In every kernel, a chuckle is found,
Nourishing minds with each silly round.

Nature's Hidden Lessons

In every crack of earth, a lesson is heard,
From ants in a line to an errant bird.
The daisies declare, 'Oh, isn't it grand?'
While the moss chuckles softly, taking a stand.

Squirrels exchange tales of nuts they have stashed,
Their laughs intertwining, as autumn is flashed.
Frogs croak in chorus, a merry little band,
With jokes in their throats, making tales quite grand.

The clouds play a game, passing shadows on trees,
While the grasshoppers hop, filled with giggles and ease.
Every rustle of leaves holds a punchline so neat,
As the dirt winks back, bringing laughter to feet.

In this realm of the wild, there's wisdom so true,
With nature as teacher, there's always a clue.
Let's wander together, and pause to unveil,
The funny adventures that life can entail.

The Blooming of Awareness

In a garden of thoughts, strange blooms arise,
With whispers of wisdom that tickle the skies.
Petals of laughter, they dance with delight,
While bees buzz with gossip from morning till night.

The veggies debate in their patchy attire,
'Tomatoes are fruits, and we're not a liar!'
A carrot slips jokes, while the radish turns red,
In the soil of the mind, the humor is spread.

As sunbeams of insight warm the fresh earth,
Each sprout tells a tale of its quirky birth.
Compost of giggles adds flavor to growth,
In this circus of flora, we ponder our troth.

So pause in the garden, take stock of the jest,
In the blooms of awareness, we find our best fest.

Nurtured by Silence

In stillness we gather, where echoes are few,
Baking thoughts in the oven, not knowing what's new.
The whispers of silence, they tickle the ear,
In this quiet escape, all the chuckles appear.

A squirrel tells secrets as he munches on nuts,
While leaves share their jokes, 'We're not just mere cuts!'
The potting shed chuckles with tales of the past,
Where beams of the sun are the humorists cast.

In silence, the blooms peek, in colors so bright,
They giggle at shadows, a playful sight!
When silence is nurtured, a bloom comes to play,
Unveiling the laughter that brightens the day.

So let's cherish the hush, let the quiet amuse,
For laughter can sprout where we most rarely choose.

The Well of Authentic Voices

Deep in the forest, where echoes collide,
Lies a well of true voices, so clear, so wide.
Each splash of the water tells stories anew,
Of frogs with ambitions and fish making do.

A turtle claims wisdom, 'I've seen it all, mate!'
While a wise old owl hoots, 'Don't underestimate!'
They croon out their tales, all quirky and bright,
Dancing through moonbeams, they bring sheer delight.

The critters convene for a night full of cheer,
With melodies rising that tickle the ear.
Each note from the well is a giggle so grand,
In authenticity's flow, we all take a stand.

So gather 'round critters, and listen with glee,
For laughter and truth flow eternally free!

Fertility of the Mind

Oh, the garden of thoughts, so messy and wild,
Where ideas sprout freely, like a rambunctious child.
We plant some odd notions and water with jokes,
While daisies debate what is funny or folks.

A pumpkin declares, 'I'm the king on this patch!'
While sunflowers giggle, 'We're destined to hatch!'
The soil, rich with humor, grows laughter like weed,
In this fertile terrain, all our dreams intercede.

When thoughts take a walk in the sun's golden rays,
They frolic like children in wild, wacky ways.
With puns on their lips, and a sparkle in eye,
This harvest of mirth makes the spirits fly high.

So embrace the madness, let your mind be unconfined,
In this garden of giggles, find what you unwind!

Embracing the Unknown

In a garden of quirks, we plant a thought,
Beneath the surface, surprises are caught.
With a shovel of laughter, we dig down deep,
What will sprout next? It's a secret to keep.

Oh, the gnomes are gossiping, what a delight,
While daisies are dancing, they're ready to fight.
With roots tangled up in some wild twist and turn,
We embrace the unknown—let the wacky meet burn.

Potatoes in tuxes, they're ready to shine,
Waving their leaves like they're sipping on wine.
Joking with mushrooms, they're quite a few jokes,
As they all grow together, these zany folks.

So here's to the chaos, the fun, and the mess,
In the garden of life, we just love to guess.
With humor as sunlight, we bloom without fear,
And chuckle at all the wild things that appear.

Finding Clarity in Chaos

Amidst the tangle of weeds, I confess,
A petunia just winked—what a floral distress!
Polka-dot daisies are planning a spree,
While roses debate who'll swing from the tree.

The sunflowers gossip, with heads held up high,
"Did you hear what the carrots said? Oh my!"
With chaos around, it's a comedy show,
Nature's own sitcom, with laughs in tow.

In this muddle of green, I find sweet reprieve,
The broccoli's dancing, you wouldn't believe.
Amidst all the chaos, a giggle erupts,
And in such pure nonsense, the wisdom disrupts.

So here's to the mayhem, the laughter we seek,
Like weeds in the garden, it's funny, not bleak.
In ruffled up petals and jokes that are free,
Clarity rises, like roots from a tree.

From the Earth Up

Digging in dirt with a spoon and a grin,
Whispers of laughter, let the fun begin!
The mint sprigs are teasing, "We're better than you!"
While the radishes laugh, "We might stink, but it's true!"

From the earth upwards, we sprout with a cheer,
Toot the horn like a beet, make the neighbors all leer.
A cabbage in shades that would challenge a clown,
Filming a series called 'Down Goes the Brown!'

Tall stalks of corn are engaged in a race,
As butterflies gasp at the frantic pace.
"Let's make this a dance-off!" a sprout yells with zest,
And the beans all reply, "We could use a good jest!"

Emerging from soil, what a curious crew,
In this joyful garden, there's always a new.
From the humble to silly, together they grow,
With laughter, they rise, putting on quite the show!

A Symphony of Growth

In the orchestra of blooms, the petals unite,
The daisies are singing, what a glorious sight!
The trumpet of tulips plays sweet on the breeze,
While the mint joins the chorus with such ease.

A cheeky old oak croons a deep, bumpy tone,
With roots tapping rhythms, they're never alone.
The peas in their pods giggle under their shell,
As they sway to the symphony, ringing a bell.

Under this canopy, plants riff with delight,
A zany concerto unfolding each night.
With whispers and chuckles, the garden's alive,
In this messy melody, funny vibes thrive.

So here's to the harmony, wildly entwined,
In nature's own symphony, fun you will find.
From blossom to laughter, the seasons compose,
In the rhythm of growth, hilarity flows!

The Garden of Realization

In a patch where funny stories grow,
Laughter blooms, and bubbles flow.
The daisies gossip, the roses giggle,
While sunflowers dance and bees do wiggle.

Worms wear glasses, checking their books,
While rabbits play chess, with serious looks.
A wise old tree shares tales of delight,
As the moon peeks in to join the night.

In this garden, no truth is exact,
Just funny moments, that's a fact.
With every twist, a chuckle is born,
And every thorn is a life reborn.

So come and munch on the laughter spread,
Where every bloom is a joke that's said.
In the soil of joy, we'll grow anew,
In the garden of truth, we'll find our hue.

Honest Light in Twilight

As daylight fades, the truth takes a bow,
The fireflies blink, and dance somehow.
A frog in a tuxedo croaks with flair,
While shadows replay the quirks of the air.

The stars crack jokes, one by one,
About the ants who thought they could run.
Every twinkle's a laugh, bright as can be,
In this playful scene, come join me!

A sunset whispers secrets of night,
With humor wrapped in its lovely light.
As the day departs, the chuckles do rise,
Painting the canvas of twilight skies.

So let's toast with fireflies under the moon,
For in this odd light, we all share a tune.
Each laugh is a spark, each giggle a ray,
In the twilight's embrace, let's dance and play.

Buds of Perception

In the spring, the buds stretch and sway,
Making funny faces, come what may.
With leaves chattering, they share their dreams,
And giggles ripple in trickling streams.

Bees in sunglasses buzz with style,
While flowers pose and flirt for a while.
The petals tease colors, bold and bright,
Making fun of the sun, oh what a sight!

Those wise little toads croak silly lines,
While ants wear hats as they toast with wines.
In this garden of smiles, perceptions ignite,
A comedy show in the soft morning light.

So let's join the buds, in this merry spree,
Where laughter sprouts, wild and free.
In the language of joy, we find our way,
Unfolding our quirks as we dance and play.

Nature's Unfolding Whisper

A breeze tells stories of mishaps galore,
Where trees laugh at squirrels and what they adore.
The clouds craft shadows that tickle the ground,
With whispers of humor all around.

Rabbits wear glasses, pretending to read,
While worms share gossip of their underground creed.
Each bud creates mischief, makes room for delight,
As critters join in on the laughter of night.

The sun winks down, and the flowers sway,
In this dance of whimsy, who'll lead the way?
The grass tickles toes in a playful embrace,
As nature unfolds its comic grace.

So listen closely to the whispers at play,
In this world of fun, join the frolic today.
For every giggle carries a secret or two,
In the heart of creation, joy shines through.

Insights in the Garden

In the garden, things are spry,
Worms wear glasses, oh my, oh my!
Plants gossip under the sun,
'What do you think? We're all just fun!'

The daisies dance, so carefree,
They say, 'We're blooms, not just debris!'
Bees are wearing tiny hats,
Buzzing jokes, like chattering chats!

When veggies meet for a chat,
'Let's pickle this, what do you say, brat?'
Tomatoes wink with a cheeky grin,
While carrots claim, 'We're where it's at!'

So if you wander in this maze,
Watch out for sprouts in playful phase,
For wisdom sprouts with a silly face,
In this garden of glee, we find our place.

The Nature of Realization

In the meadow, thoughts take flight,
Grass blades chat through day and night.
'Have you heard the daffodils laugh?
They think they're as tall as the giraffe!'

A squirrel claims to know it all,
'Life's a ball, just take a fall!'
With acorns bouncing in the trees,
He lifts his tail, 'Look at me, please!'

Clouds drift by, all fluffy and white,
'We float with dreams, isn't it bright?'
They tickle the sun, then dive away,
While raindrops grumble, 'What a play!'

So come and join this quirky crew,
Where sunlight dances and skies are blue,
And laughter blooms in every glade,
In nature's jest, the truth is laid.

The Roots of the Matter

Deep down low, where critters poke,
Roots are whispering, 'Aren't we woke?'
'We anchor dreams,' one vine does state,
'And all that matters starts with fate!'

In the soil, they're having fun,
'We're the underground, we've already won!'
They chuckle as they twist and bend,
'They think they know us, let's pretend!'

Dandelions plot with leafy glee,
'We'll burst in laughter, just wait and see!'
A thistle jokes, 'I'm prickly but wise,'
And everyone giggles beneath the skies.

So underfoot, the truth is spun,
With every giggle, a root is run,
In this tangled mess where wisdom flows,
Life's the punchline, and everybody knows!

Sprouts of Understanding

Tiny shoots peek from the ground,
Getting taller, what a sound!
'Hey there, buddy, what's your plan?'
'I'm sprouting wisdom, don't be bland!'

Buds are bursting with jokes to share,
A radish claims it's quite a rare flair,
While peas in pods all crack up loud,
'We're the funniest in the crowd!'

Sunflower turns to say, 'Look here!'
'Life's a garden, full of cheer!'
With each bloom hugs, they spread delight,
Twisting truths, both day and night.

So when in doubt, just sprout a smile,
And laughter carries for a country mile,
In every nudge and playful tease,
Understanding's dance is sure to please.

Roots of Revelation

In the garden of my mind, I plant,
A thought so wild, it makes me rant.
With quirky roots that twist and tease,
They giggle softly in the breeze.

I water them with jokes and puns,
As laughter dances, sidesteps and runs.
Fertilized by wonder, they grow so spry,
Revealing truths that make me cry.

Each sprout a tale, absurd and bright,
With revelations that tickle with delight.
I prune the doubts, let humor bloom,
My garden's a circus, dispelling the gloom.

So come take a look, don't be shy,
In this quirky land, where thoughts fly high
With roots like these, what can go wrong?
Join the laughter, it's where we belong!

Blossoms of Hidden Wisdom

Blossoms peek from behind the fence,
With giggles wrapped in sweet suspense.
They hold the secrets, bright and cute,
Winking at passersby in their pursuit.

Each petal whispers a joke or two,
About the world and what we do.
They flicker in colors of vibrant cheer,
Dropping wisdom wrapped up in a sneer.

With a playful flick, they catch the breeze,
As funny phrases dance with ease.
Watch them sway, these wise little sprites,
Guiding us gently through glorious nights.

So let them teach you to laugh and grin,
In every blossom, where truth begins.
Embrace the silliness, let it spring,
From hidden wisdom, let's all take wing!

Fertile Grounds of Understanding

In fields of jest where answers sprout,
The ground shakes up with a jovial shout.
We plant our thoughts, a comedic lot,
Harvesting giggles in every plot.

Digging deeper for the punchline's gold,
As laughter echoes, never grows old.
The soil is rich with crazy ideas,
We water them down with reflective cheers.

The crops of laughter rise from the muck,
Yielding insights, oh so plucky luck.
With every chuckle, the yield outgrows,
The bounty of wisdom that foolishly glows.

So let's dance in this fertile space,
Where understanding wears a funny face.
On these grounds, all must cultivate,
The giggling truths that can't wait!

Echoes from the Underground

Down below where the giggles dwell,
In tunnels of humor, secrets swell.
Echoes bounce off the roots and rock,
Telling tales in a whimsical walk.

With each muffled laugh, new truths arise,
Tickling ears with their clever surprise.
From underground springs, wisdom flows,
Spritzing up laughs, where mischief glows.

They whisper softly, these curious sprouts,
Exchanging jokes where the dark flouts.
In hidden corners, they plot and scheme,
Echoes from below, a zany dream.

So heed the whispers, low and bright,
From subterranean realms, take flight.
The echoes call with a cheeky grin,
Join the laughter, let the fun begin!

The Light Within the Grove

In the grove where shadows play,
The sun sneaks in a funny way,
With squirrels plotting silly tricks,
While trees giggle—nature's fix.

A rabbit hops to catch a ray,
While birds chirp in a jaunty sway,
Each leaf a wink, each branch a joke,
Laughter blooms where wisdom spoke.

The mushrooms dance beneath the trees,
In their top hats, feeling breezy,
They twirl and spin, no care abounds,
In this wacky world, joy resounds.

So wander here with an open mind,
What seems absurd, the truth may find,
For laughter hides where roots extend,
In every glance, we twist and bend.

Mysterious Weaving

In the garden, threads entwine,
A spider hums a silly line,
With every weave, a tale unfurls,
Of hidden jokes in leafy swirls.

The daisies gossip, oh so bright,
About the night and moon's delight,
They weave together stories grand,
Of laughter spun by nature's hand.

A gopher digs without a care,
Unraveling truth from underground lair,
He pauses, snickers at the chase,
"For wisdom's found in goofy grace!"

So in this place, with threads so green,
The funniest tales are oft unseen,
A tapestry of chuckles grow,
Mysterious weaving—come and go.

The Riddle of Growth

A sprout asked roots, "Why so deep?"
The roots just laughed, "We're on a leap!"
With each stretch, they play hopscotch,
"Let's make it fun!" they joyfully botch.

"Do you think we'll find a sprout?"
A leaf replied with no doubt,
"But what's the point if we can't giggle?"
The plants agreed, "Let's shake and wiggle!"

As flowers bloom with colors bold,
They shout and sing, "Let's break the mold!"
With bees that buzz a silly tune,
The garden laughs beneath the moon.

The riddle teased, "What will it be?"
"Let's grow together, you and me!"
With roots and laughs, we sprout and sway,
In this wild dance of every day.

Cultivating Awareness

In the field where the veggies grin,
A carrot jokes, "Let the fun begin!"
With dirt and giggles, off they glow,
"Plant a thought, see what will grow!"

The wise old onion, peeling charm,
"Awareness sprouts, you'll come to harm,
If you can't laugh at what you see,
Join the dance, it's key to be free!"

Tomatoes chime in, round and red,
"Who knew that truth hid 'neath the shed?"
With humor bright as morning dew,
They cultivate joy in every hue.

So plant a dream, don't take a fall,
In this patch of laughter, we stand tall,
For when we learn through silly cheer,
Awareness blooms, both bright and clear.

Buried Gems of Understanding

In the soil of silly thoughts,
Funny ideas sprout like weeds,
Wiggling worms in laughter dance,
Planting truths among the seeds.

Digging deep with shovels bright,
Comedic roots twist and twirl,
Uncovering odd nuggets now,
A treasure chest of giggles swirl.

With every poke, a chuckle bursts,
Who knew learning could be fun?
Finding blushing coco-nutts,
Underneath the shining sun!

So let's harvest joy today,
From the goofy garden's lore,
Where wisdom sprouts with such delight,
And laughter blooms forevermore.

The Dance of the Garden

In the garden where jokes collide,
Blooms of laughter twist and sway,
Petals pirouette in the breeze,
Comedic puns come out to play.

Bees are buzzing songs of cheer,
While gophers moonwalk on their paws,
Flowers chuckle, roots tap dance,
Nature's show, with playful cause.

A carrot sports a silly hat,
Radishes in gowns parade,
Every leaf has a punchline stored,
In this green escapade.

Gather 'round, it's dinner time,
With veggies dressed for fun,
In this garden full of humor,
Laughter flows like a running pun.

Rains of Revelation

Raindrops fall, a tickle on heads,
Each drop a giggle from above,
Soaking thoughts in joyful streams,
Revealing wisdom wrapped in love.

Puddles gather, splashing smiles,
Rubber boots stomp with delight,
Each splash a lesson in disguise,
Dancing truths on a rainy night.

Clouds release their secrets, bright,
A thunderous roar of laughter flows,
Worms rejoice in muddy glee,
As nature's humor truly grows.

Dry off now with sunny rays,
The sky smiles, no need to pout,
With every storm, there's joy to find,
In the downpour, laughs come out.

Seasonal Truths

Springtime giggles burst anew,
With silly blooms in vivid hue,
Flowers tease the buzzing bees,
Making honeyed jokes with ease.

Summer sun invites a laugh,
Watermelons split in half,
Juicy jokes drip down like juice,
In this circus, no excuse.

Autumn leaves begin to jest,
Falling down, they take a rest,
Crisp air filled with pumpkin glee,
Stories rustle in each tree.

Winter's frost brings chilly fun,
Snowballs fly, a playful run,
With every season, joy's the plan,
Nature laughs, hand in hand.

The Blooming Mind

In the garden of quirky thoughts,
I plant my ideas like little pots.
Some grow tall, while others flop,
But each one gives a giggle and a hop.

A daisy laughs, a rose winks bright,
They bump and chat, it's quite the sight.
With every bloom, a punchline blooms,
Nature's jesters in colorful costumes.

Worms get giggly, ants start to dance,
They think it's their time for a prance.
The sun shines down with a sunny grin,
Laughing along as the antics begin.

So let each thought sprout wild and free,
In this garden where silliness is the key.
With each new idea that bursts in my mind,
I'll cultivate joy, whimsical and unconfined.

Fragments of Enlightenment

In the attic of nonsense, I found my muse,
A potato in a hat wearing purple shoes.
It whispered wisdom, or maybe a pun,
About how laughter comes in when work is done.

A split pea laughed at a tattered book,
Said, "I'm sprouting knowledge, come take a look!"
With every chuckle, a thought took wing,
In this circus of phrases, I hear them sing.

The light bulb flickers, then starts to sway,
As the parsnip four-steps and steals the day.
A broccoli's jest becomes legendary lore,
In this festival of insight, who could ask for more?

Fragments of laughter are scattered about,
In the compost of wisdom, we twist and shout.
Each quirky notion, a vibrant thread,
Binding us together, with glee, we're fed.

Nature's Vocal Chords

In the symphony of leaves, I hear a tune,
A squirrel croons softly to the afternoon.
The flowers join in with a rustling sound,
Making melodies where silliness abounds.

The daisies hum sweet, while the thistles screech,
With pollen as confetti, they dance and preach.
The trees sway, their branches like arms,
Joining in harmony, with all of their charms.

A bumblebee buzzes, looking for rhyme,
As bunnies hop along with perfect time.
Each critter has rhythm, a part to play,
In nature's own chorus, come join the fray!

So here's to the laughter that nature imparts,
With vocal chords made of petals and hearts.
Tune into the giggles, the chuckles, the cheer,
In the concert of growth, the truth is quite clear.

The Language of Flora

Petals chatter in breezy delight,
As the sun dips low and turns off the light.
A tulip tells tales of its high-flying friends,
While daisies droop, dreaming of weekend trends.

The violets gossip about who's new,
A cactus chimes in, "Don't forget about dew!"
With every soft whisper, a jest slips by,
In this garden of banter, we giggle and sigh.

The daisies form circles, playing charades,
While sunflowers pose like fashion parades.
Grass blades grow tall, trying to eavesdrop,
Chickweed chuckles, "You'll never get top!"

In this botanical bar, humor is free,
With every petal, there's a new memory.
So let's share these tales of flora and glee,
For laughter is the language that sets us all free.

Growth from Darkness

In the soil where shadows creep,
Little whispers start to leap,
Worms throw parties in the gloom,
While daisies plot their grand costume.

Sunlight laughs, it breaks the night,
Plants stretch up with all their might,
But in the dark, they dance and play,
Making shadows join the fray.

Pinecones giggle, acorns tease,
They hitch a ride on gentle breeze,
Each sprout a jester, bright and spry,
Turning dirt into a pie.

From muck and mire, a tale unfurls,
Where laughter blooms and chaos swirls,
In every gloom, a joy to share,
Nature's jesters, unaware!

Unveiling Nature's Stories

In every leaf, a tale is spun,
From buzzing bees to rivers run,
Whispers carried on the air,
Telling secrets, do we dare?

A squirrel's antics, quite absurd,
Dancing 'round without a word,
His acorn stash, a comedy,
While all the trees roll branches, whee!

A clever crow with witty caws,
Picks through rubbish, finds applause,
Each worm a witness to the play,
As nature winks, "Just another day!"

Rustling grasses, laughter soft,
A rabbit jumps and shakes it off,
Between the cracks and every bend,
Nature's snares may just offend!

Roots of Belief

In the garden of quirky thoughts,
Roots wiggle like they've missed their shots,
One thinks he's grand, a kingly show,
While others below just laugh and grow.

Tangled truths, a snarl of doubt,
Each twist and turn, a playful rout,
"Who's the sage?" one root proclaims,
While vines below are playing games!

With laughter bubbling in the dirt,
Tiny critters winked and flirt,
Mycelium spreads its jokes galore,
The underground keeps wanting more!

In tangled webs of laughter here,
Beliefs take root, then disappear,
For every doubt, a giggle's planted,
In soil where the light is slanted!

The Fertile Ground of Understanding

In hearts and minds, a plot is made,
Where wisdom dances, unafraid,
With spades of laughter, seeds are sown,
Each chuckle breaks the heavy stone.

Together we dig through muck and clay,
And shout absurdities along the way,
Planting questions, watering dreams,
Creating giggles, or so it seems.

A cactus jokes, a rose retorts,
"Grow your humor without any shorts!"
Ripe apples swinging from branches high,
With every pluck, a snicker, oh my!

In the chaos of growing pains,
Understanding laughs through bright refrains,
Let's build a world where 'fun' is found,
In the fertile earth, where jokes abound!

Nature's Quiet Revelations

In the garden, a squirrel hops,
Chasing shadows, and falling crops.
A worm wriggles, in jovial glee,
Singing songs of the bumblebee.

A turtle pondered, slow and wise,
While ants marched by with tiny pies.
The daisies giggle in the breeze,
Whispering secrets to the trees.

A rain cloud grumbles, full of cheer,
Splashing puddles for all to hear.
The sun peeked out and cracked a smile,
Sparking joy for just a while.

In laughter's echo, truths unwind,
Nature's quirks, delightfully blind.
With every quirk, the woods relay,
Life's funny truth in a playful way.

Truths Buried in Earth

Beneath the surface, what a find,
A gopher's stash, quite unrefined.
He burrows deep, with snacks galore,
Planting chips—a feast in store.

The quicksand's quip, a clumsy step,
As frogs leap in with a loud 'Yep!'
A beetle rolls a ball of pride,
Wishing it was a big slide ride.

Potatoes wear their jackets tight,
Ready for a waltz every night.
The carrots tease, with leafy crowns,
Waving humor in golden gowns.

From roots to fruits, the fun is ripe,
Each little sprout has its own type.
Nature laughs at the quirky mess,
Buried truths in the earth's caress.

Echoes of the Heart's Soil

In soil's embrace, jokes are cracked,
As daisies pull a prank—that's a fact!
The breeze sneezes, leaves take flight,
All while the sun says, 'What a sight!'

The heart of the land beats so bold,
With giggles dug in stories old.
Mice host parties inside their holes,
While crickets tune their midnight roles.

A lonely cactus wants a friend,
Poking fun till the day's end.
While shadows dance with blushing blooms,
Echoing laughter that brightly zooms.

So let's unearth a smile or two,
In every patch, a whiff of dew.
Nature's humor, a joyful blend,
Reminds us all —there's fun to send!

Hidden Wisdom in Bloom

Petals whisper secrets in the air,
Pansies giggle without a care.
Blooming tales of a bumble's quest,
Nature's humor—a vibrant jest.

Lilies wear their polka dots,
Playing dress-up with happy thoughts.
A tulip slips, the others cheer,
Each flower laughing, loud and clear.

In vineyards where the grapes doth sway,
A vine tells jokes at the end of day.
The sun rolls back, gives a wink,
While the berries blush—oh, what a link!

Hidden truths in whimsical guise,
Blooms bursting forth, a grand surprise.
With every laugh that nature shares,
Wisdom blooms in funny airs.

Fables of the Forgotten Earth

In the garden of whispers, where rumors sprout,
The carrots gossip loud, what's that all about?
The radishes chuckle, they wear silly hats,
While the peas in their pods, discuss where it's at.

The flowers plot mischief, with petals so bright,
They're scheming a dance under the pale moonlight.
The worms spin tall tales, of daring escape,
While the snails take their time, in a sticky, slow shape.

Beneath the old tree, the creatures convene,
With all of their giggles, it's quite the scene.
The sun gives a wink, and the shadows all cheer,
For the laughter of nature is music to hear.

So remember the fables of this forgotten place,
Where the soil knows secrets, and grows with a grace.
For in every small seed, a story is spun,
And the humor of life is a dance always fun.

Petals of Perception

In a field of bright colors, there's plenty to see,
The daisies are waving, and laughing with glee.
The roses are bloomin', but don't be misled,
They're plotting a prank since a few bees they fed.

The tulips are chatting, with winds in their hair,
About how the daisies are lacking their flair.
The sunflowers tower, look down with disdain,
Saying, "You're all foolish, oh what a domain!"

Beneath all the chatter, new notions will burst,
Like petals in spring, ideas will thirst.
A daffodil grins, "The fun is in view,"
As they swap silly tales with a touch of dew.

When perception blooms, oh the laughter it brings,
Nature's own court where the whimsy still sings.
So join in the banter, let smiles be your guide,
In this garden of giggles, let joy be your pride.

The Harvest of Ideas

In the field of thick thoughts, the crops start to grow,
With pumpkins debating how big they will go.
The corn stalks are plotting some wild party tricks,
While the beets roll their eyes, saying, "Give it a mix!"

Grapes hang in clusters, with juicy tales told,
Of the gopher who tried to be brave and bold.
With cackles of laughter, the squash join along,
In harmony chattering their own silly song.

The carrots get sassy, they boast of their crunch,
While the peppers dance wildly, they're craving a bunch.
They say wit is the fruit, the most prized of the lot,
And it seems with each harvest, those ideas are hot!

So gather your bounty, let humor take root,
In this delightful patch, give laughter a shoot.
For the harvest of jest is the sweetest of yields,
And the spirit of jesting in fun is our shield.

Revelations in the Earth

Underneath the old oak, secrets dance with the breeze,
The moles share confessions as they wiggle with ease.
With mushrooms as hats, the toads might confess,
"How is it we're all such a glorious mess?"

The insects host parties, with music and cheer,
While the ants carry tidbits, reminders so near.
A goofy old tortoise spits wisdom with glee,
"Life's a riddle, my friends, so come laugh with me!"

The roots weave together, their stories entwined,
Each planted notion, whimsical and kind.
With a nod from the daisies, they wink and they sway,
Today's quirky truth is tomorrow's bouquet.

So dive into laughter, let quirks be your worth,
For the revelations sprouting from deep in the earth,
Are bundles of joy, in their nature so free,
With every odd joke, be the best you can be!

www.ingramcontent.com/pod-product-compliance
Lightning Source LLC
Chambersburg PA
CBHW071836160426
43209CB00003B/317